Alternative Medicine for Pets

Your Guide to Holistic Health for your Dog and Cat

Jackie Gee

Alternative Medicine for Pets – Your Guide to Holistic Health for your Dog and Cat by Jackie Gee Copyright 2015

All rights reserved. No part of this publication may be reproduced, stored in a retrieval system, or transmitted, in any form or by any means, electronic, mechanical, photocopying, recording, or otherwise, without prior written permission from the publisher.

This e-book may not be re-sold or re-printed without permission. If you wish to share this e-book with another person, please purchase an additional copy of the book for each person you wish to share it with.

If you are reading this e-book and did not purchase it, or it was not purchased for your personal use only, then you should return it to one of the many online distributors of this electronic book and purchase your own copy.

Thank you for respecting the authors time, efforts and work.

Contents

Introduction 9
CHAPTER 1 13
Why Use Alternative Medicine for Your Pet? 13
CHAPTER 2 19
Pros and Cons of Alternate Pet Remedies: Long Term and Short Term 19
   Short-Term Effects of Alternate Medicines 19
   Long-Term Effects of Alternative Medicines 20
      Combining medicines 22
      Organic is best 22
      Allergic Reactions 23
CHAPTER 3 25
Types of Homeopathic Treatments to Use on Your Pets 25
   Flower Essences 26
   Touch Therapy 27
   Applied Kinesiology 28
   Detox 29
CHAPTER 4 33
DIET 33
   HEMP and the benefits 33
   Does Your Pet Have a Food Intolerance? 35
   Does Your Pet Have Allergies? 36
CHAPTER 5 39
FLEAS – The Pet World's Biggest Bug Bear 39
   Nontoxic Tick and Flea Control (Cats and Dogs) 39
      NEMATODES 40

BORIC ACID	40
NYLAR	41
FLEA ZAPPERS	42
FLEA TRAPS	42
CEDAR OIL	43
GARLIC and YEAST	43
FLEA PILLS	43
CHAPTER 6	45
Long- and Short-Term Ailments and How to Treat Them	45
Short-Term Ailments in Pets and How to Treat Them	45
Gastrointestinal Disorders and Digestive Problems	45
External and Internal Injuries	46
Chest Problems	47
Cold Problems	47
Dental Diseases	47
First Aid – the Herbal Way	48
How can herbs and aromatherapy help pets who suffer with allergies?	52
Long-Term Ailments in Pets and How to Treat Them	55
Arthritis and Joint Pain	55
Cancer	56
Diabetes	58
Liver and Kidney Diseases	59
Heartworm	60
Cushing Disease	60
Cognitive Dysfunction	62
Pancreatitis	62
CHAPTER 7	63

How to Approach Supplements and Natural Foods for Your Pet.
They Are What They Eat! 63
    Raw Food Diet..67
    VITAMIN 101..67
CHAPTER 8 75
Vaccines..75
    NOSODES..78
CHAPTER 9 81
So, How Effective is All This Anyway? 81
CHAPTER 10 85
Strategies for Pets with Different Ailments.....................................85

This book is dedicated to my bestie Sayoko Murase, whose love and devotion to doggies, especially her rescue pit bulls is amazing and inspiring as is her care and concern for friends. God bless.

Introduction

More and more of us look to alternative and natural remedies to cure our ailments, both long and short term, and the body of evidence is building to show that the natural way is not only safe but also effective.

In our great excitement over popping little pink and green pills as a quick fix, we have forgotten about natural remedies. Now we realize that the so-called quick fixes come with a raft of side effects and some unknown long-term problems and are not always that effective anyway.

So what's good for the goose is also good for the gander, right?
Or should I say what's good for us is also what is good for Fido and Moggy.

The majority of pet owners are faced with different challenges when looking for everything from nourishing foods, remedies for parasite infections and cures for various diseases. In relation to curing diseases and getting rid of parasitic infections, there is a lot of criticism about the use of alternative medicine to cure these ailments and completely get rid of the parasites. This leads to confusion among pet owners.

Anyone who has ever used alternative and conventional medicine, (also called traditional medicine), knows that there is a profound difference between the two. Basically, both can be used to effectively treat and cure diseases and infections in pets. Sometimes they are more effective when used together. However, the difference is clear. Conventional medicine, also called traditional medicine in this eBook, is the tried and tested medicines that are usually suggested by vets in the case of illness. Conversely, alternative medicine is a type of cure that, although it may lack a vast body of scientific evidence, is believed to have similar effects and is anecdotally popular.

Therefore as a pet owner, this is a tough decision that you have to make for the wellbeing of your pets. Your local veterinary officer may be in a better position to help you choose what's good. Many of them blend alternative and modern medicine so as to devise a proper pet care system that meets long and short terms needs.

Just like doctors, some vets are more open to alternate and holistic methods than others. Some are just stubborn and set in their ways so if you want support in pursuing the alternate route with your pet, find a vet who is progressive and helpful.

Some of the most popular therapies include:

Herbal Treatments - Involves use of plant remedies to treat a variety of ailments. One of the most common remedy for treating allergies and arthritis is alfalfas.

Homeopathy – This type of treatment is used to jumpstart the body's own healing response with some dilute substances that cause the same symptoms that the pet is suffering from.

Acupuncture - This method of treatment involves inserting fine needles into specific areas of the pet's body to balance energy flow. This treatment is used to cure chronic ailments and to control pain.

Nutritional Supplements - These natural supplements are used to control nutritional deficiencies by supplying adequate amounts of minerals, vitamins, fatty acids and amino acids. These help improve the overall health of the pet.

CHAPTER 1

Why Use Alternative Medicine for Your Pet?

There are many reasons why you should consider using alternative medicine for your pet. Alternative medicine is useful in two main ways.
- A) Treating and preventing various health problems that commonly affect pets such as dogs and cats with fewer side effects and nasty reactions.
- B) Strengthening the animals' immunity and increasing their vitality so that they stay healthier for a long time.

There are several factors that may affect a pet's health. One of them is diet. So many problems arise from the intake of different types of modern foods, even in human beings. When I was in school, I was allergic to fish and I never knew another kid who suffered from any allergy at all. Today, almost everyone I know is allergic to something. I believe it comes down to the use of highly processed foods and modern ingredients that have increased our levels of sensitivity by damaging the gut, and it is no different for pets.

Alternative medicine has long been praised for treating food-related allergies and nutritional deficiencies. Pets, like cats and dogs thrive on raw meat for survival and are therefore exposed to germs and bacteria. In this case, alternate remedies are effective for treating any diseases that may be caused by germs and bacteria, as well as those caused by allergies.

Alternate medicine is also effective in treating degenerative joint diseases such as **arthritis**. Since many pets suffer from such ailments, alternative remedies and methods can be incorporated with good diet to improve the health of the animal's joints. Anti-oxidant vitamins and Omega Fatty Acids supplements are becoming more popular as non-drug remedies for joint problems. Apart from treating arthritis, these vitamins and omega fatty acids are used to treat allergies that severely affect the pets' skin and coat.

Alternative medicine is also used by pet owners and veterinarians for **Flea and Tick control**. Chemicals used to control such pests are a major health concern because they contain harsh agents that may harm the pets. However, use of alternative medicine is risk-free and does not pose any health risk to the animals. Some of the major remedies used include herbs, garlic, and brewer's yeast. With the ongoing awareness campaigns about health problems that come with the use of chemicals to remove fleas and ticks, many pharmaceutical companies have resorted to manufacturing insecticides which contain pyrethrum. Pyrethrum is a natural insecticide made from the dried flower heads of *Chrysanthemum cinerariifolium* and *Chrysanthemum coccineum.*

Some researchers do not entirely believe in this method of treatment because such remedies may not be strong enough to control a pest infestation. Prevention is always better than cure. Spraying the pets' kennel or basket with a growth inhibitor or pyrethrum insecticide products may help prevent infestations. There are different types of **pyrethrum insecticide products** on the market today. Pyrethrum contains Pyrethrins, which are the main insecticidal compounds. These active compounds include pyrethrin I, pyrethrin II, cinerin I, cinerin II, jasmolin I, and jasmolin II. When in contact with the pests, Pyrethrins works by acting on the nervous system to provide a very quick "knockdown" which reduces their mobility and finally kills. The key disadvantage of pyrethrins is that they breakdown easily especially when exposed to the sunlight thus providing a very short residual activity. This literally means that the pests may recover and you may have to apply the Pyrethrum several times. (See Chapter 5 for more on natural tick and flea control.)

Alternative medicine can also be used to **vaccinate** pets thus helping prevent disease naturally. Some of the most common alternative vaccines are the **nosodes** (See chapter 8) which are mainly given orally. If you wish to have your pets vaccinated by use of alternative vaccines, you can visit a Holistic Veterinary Center where you will find vaccine alternatives that are completely safe for use. **These vaccines do not contain preservatives such as mercury or lead or preservatives** which are highly toxic and can cause cognitive problems. However, nosodes are not considered as the most effective method because some infections like rabies, scabies, and other communicable diseases are highly infectious, which calls for both the use of alternative and conventional vaccines to effectively control infections. (See Chapter on Vaccines)

Although **conventional vaccines** have been used successfully in the control of many diseases, they have their negative sides too. One of the common disadvantages of conventional medicine is the possible reversion to the virulent form of the live vaccines as well as the failures in the activation of inactivated vaccines. There is also the danger of contamination by an undetected bacteria or virus. They also cause various health problems such as inflammation, hypersensitivity or transitory immunosuppression.

All in all, using alternative medicine to treat diseases in your pets is not enough. Giving your pets a healthy diet is essential for overall body health and immune system boosting. Water is also very important for proper hydration and exercise for stronger body muscles.

Although alternative medicine has its place in the modern society, it cannot be entirely relied upon to cure certain diseases; despite the fact that it has helped pets to overcome a vast range of health issues. In cases like cancer, surgery and conventional medicine becomes handy. That's why as a pet owner, its important decide what's the best alternative for your pet. Often alternate medicine becomes the only solution when pet insurance will not pay out or where conventional medicine runs out of ideas or fails to diagnose properly.

On the brighter side, alternative medicine is considered as less invasive and has fewer side effects as compared to modern medicine. Alternative pet health treatment can help your pet heal, regain energy, increase overall vitality and prolong life.

Alternative medicine, especially natural herbs, can provide pets with the vitality they need to live for many years. This is one big advantage because as a pet owner, you are likely to pay less cash to your local vet for treatment, because alternative medicine is cheap and readily available. On the other hand, you are more likely to face massive bills when treating your pet with conventional treatment methods like surgery. As with humans, for alternate pet care to be effective it should be part of a holistic health plan for your pet –

nutritious eating, exercise, plenty of water and nutritional supplements including herbs.

However, if your pet is at a high risk of contracting chronic illnesses and injuries, it is advisable that you choose one or more insurance policy for security purposes.

There are many products available today which have proven to be useful in meeting your pets' health needs. They are readily available and certainly effective.

CHAPTER 2

Pros and Cons of Alternate Pet Remedies: Long Term and Short Term

Before trying out any type of alternative medicine, it's always good to consider the advantages and disadvantages. Basically, it's important to take extra caution when using any medications. Alternative medicines can harm your pets severely if improperly used. There are many positive sides of these types of medicines, however nothing is 100% effective and safe. Here is what you need to know about short-term and long-term effects of common alternate cures.

Short-Term Effects of Alternate Medicines

Incorrect use of alternative medicine can result in various negative side effects. It's always good to follow a veterinarian's advice on how to properly administer the medicine. For example, a **Vitamin A and Hypervitaminosis D** overdose can lead to severe dehydration, hair loss, and even vomiting.

The use of herbs to cure certain skin problems can have some side effects. For example, **Valerian** is a herb used for its sedative effects and can be used if your dog has anxiety or is highly strung. However, high doses may cause gastrointestinal discomfort. **Garlic** is used in treatment of microbial infections, treatment of parasites, as well as that of cancer. However, it might cause Heinz body anemia in dogs. Therefore, it should not be used to treat pets suffering from anemia. **Acupuncture** also has several side-effects which are usually normal. They include bleeding, bruising, pain, and soreness.

Alternate medicine interacts with other drugs and this may lead to severe side-effects. For example, **Cranberry,** which is used to support and maintain a healthy urinary tract, may cause bleeding when it interacts with other drugs. These drugs include Warfarin (Coumadin and Jantoven), Miradon, Aisindione, and Dicumarol. Warfarin may cause severe bleeding, red/brown stool, headaches and stomachache, joint pains, swelling, and discomfort after injury, vomiting blood, as well as dizziness and general body weakness.

Other short-term effects of using alternative medicine on pets include gastrointestinal disturbances, dizziness, dry mouth, allergic reactions, photosensitivity, fatigue, seizures, diarrhea etc.

Away from herbal medicine, supplements and their effects on the pets, other types of alternative medicinal therapies may also have some effects. **Acupuncture** has many positive effects and negative ones too. Although the effects in pets are less noticeable, they are worth knowing about for the safety of your pet. After the session, your pet may experience bruising at needled areas, soreness, muscle twitching, as well as fatigue. These effects usually go away after a short period and do not pose a threat to your pet's long-term health.

Long-Term Effects of Alternative Medicines

As it is with all types of medicines, alternative medicine has some long-term effects too, especially if administered over a long period of time. Thus, it's important to monitor your pet's health to reduce the risk of toxicity and other harmful effects. Here are the long-term effects of certain alternative medicines which can potentially harm your pet.

Vitamin A overdose can lead to vitamin toxicity in the pet's body which may result in liver problems and osteoporosis.
Hypervitaminosis D overdose leads to kidney stones which can be fatal.

Likewise, some herbs are also harmful to the pet's health. The problem with most people is that they believe that alternative medicines such as herbs are natural and thereby safe for use. However, this is not necessarily so because sometimes the herb itself can have adverse side effects. In other cases, these herbs may interact with conventional medicine increasing the risks of severe side effects when used with certain drugs. Here are some of the herbs that may have long-term impacts on the pet's health:

Pennyroyal is a herb containing essential oils. It is used to treat and control fleas and ticks in dogs, cats, and horses. It is used as an insecticide and is extremely toxic to dogs and cats in high doses. The essential oil in the herb is very concentrated and should not be used on dogs and cats, especially if they have an existing kidney condition or are pregnant.

Undiluted Tea Tree Oil is a popular alternative treatment for skin conditions affecting both humans and pets. However, it is extremely toxic when ingested orally. The animal may appear weak and have difficulties when walking. Cats especially, are highly sensitive to essential oils and they should not be used on them. All essential oils should be safely stored away from pets.

Comfrey is a natural skin healer that reduces inflammation when applied to the skin. However, comfrey contains small quantities of alkaloids that cause cancer and liver damage if taken in large quantities or if used for a prolonged period.

Yucca is a medicinal plant that is widely used for its anti-inflammatory and anti-arthritic properties. It is used in treatment of both Osteoarthritis and Rheumatoid arthritis. However, large doses of Yucca can irritate the stomach lining as well as the intestinal mucosa. This may cause vomiting and bloating. It's only safe when used in smaller doses.

Wormwood is a traditional de-worming herb that contains strong volatile oils and tannins as well as bitter principles. Due to this reason, wormwood can cause liver and kidney problems, and in extreme cases, it can damage the nervous system. Veterinarian advice is essential in this case.

Garlic is used to treat microbial infections, parasites such as fleas and worms, and also in the treatment of cancer. However when used in large amounts, garlic can cause Heinz body anemia in cats and dogs. Therefore, proper testing before use is highly recommended. It should not be used on pets suffering from anemia because it may exacerbate the condition.

Other not-so-serious side effects of herbs are diarrhea, vomiting, sneezing, swelling and runny nose and eyes.

Combining medicines

When used with modern medicine, alternative medicine may cause drug interactions that may badly affect the pet's internal organs. Supplements and herbs interact with prescription and over-the-counter medication. A lot of care should be taken when administering these drugs together. Get advice when combining medications as certain alternate and modern medications used together can cause long-term sicknesses like kidney stones, gastrointestinal diseases which can be difficult to treat, cardiovascular diseases, and in extreme cases, they may cause infertility in pets. Some of the most commonly affected systems include cardiovascular, renal, neurological, hematologic, endocrine, and pulmonary.

Organic is best

When using alternate and herbal remedies you want to be sure that they are of a high quality and are organic if possible, if not they may do your pet more harm than good in the long term. Contamination is a repeated problem due to the fact that some raw plant materials may be contaminated with microorganisms such as fungi and other bacteria. There is also the possibility that the herbal remedies are contaminated with pesticide residues. Others are heavily contaminated with heavy metals such as lead, mercury, arsenic, and cadmium. These raw materials may cause adverse effects on the pet's health. Therefore, it's highly advisable that you buy these products from licensed dealers who are reputable. It is also important to check the packaging of the products; broken seals or decay in the case of raw plant materials may make them unsafe for use.

Allergic Reactions

The use of natural supplements may not augur well with the body's immune system and may therefore cause severe bodily reactions such as allergies. Examples of the supplements that can cause allergic reactions include milk thistle, flaxseed, ginseng, echinacea, saw palmetto, garlic, St. John's wort, phytoestrogens (dong quai, soy, and black cohosh), ginko biloba, kava, and many others.

Therefore, it's important to give the correct dosages of the medicine to your pets to avoid further complications. Also, it's highly advisable to obtain the best quality medicine there is from trustworthy suppliers.

CHAPTER 3

Types of Homeopathic Treatments to Use on Your Pets

Before you read about the three types of homeopathic treatments to use on your pets, it's important for you to know the real meaning of homeopathic treatment. Homeopathy is the a medical practice which treats a disease by administration of minute doses of a remedy that would in large amounts produce in healthy person's symptoms similar to those of the disease.

In animals, homeopathic treatment is no different from that of human beings. Although there are different types of homeopathic treatments that you can use on your pets, the most recommended ones are Flower Essences, Touch Therapy, Applied Kinesiology, and Detox.

Most veterinarians treat any disease symptoms with prescriptions of expensive, patented toxic pharmaceuticals. These dangerous prescription medications are used to treat and cure cancer, arthritis, diabetes, and even heart diseases. However today, a growing number of veterinarians around the world are turning to homeopathic remedies for the treatment of many animal problems. They range from cancer, arthritis, allergic reactions as well as other chronic illnesses.

This type of treatment is readily available, safe to use on all animals and an effective alternative to conventional veterinary practice. Below is a detailed explanation of three types of homeopathic treatments and their effectiveness.

Flower Essences

This is a type of homeopathic treatment where flower essences are used to promote the healing process. Flower essences are liquid preparations that contain minute traces of actual flowers, which generally convey a vibrational pattern and the essence of specific flowers. It is because of this reason that their actions are not biochemical but vibrational, which means that they are subtle and extend beyond the physiological.

Flower essences have a reputation of being safe for both humans and animals. According to research, there is an interrelationship between physical illness, stress and emotional outlook. Pets experience many positive changes after the therapy because flower essences address issues which often belie stress and various other health problems. Basically, they help release emotional energetic knots.

Flower essences help transform attitudes, emotions, and patterns of behavior to enhance development, growth, and awareness.

A professional homeopathic vet takes several things into account before administering the treatment. First, treatment is based on the severity of the symptoms, which include both physical and emotional. Also, treatment is based on whether any underlying health problems are manifesting themselves as a result of existing emotional issues.

The first step is to start with an alternate remedy, then evaluate the results, and finally, incorporate flower essences into the therapy.

Use of flower essences on pets is very useful because it promotes physical and emotional healing by changing emotional and behavioral patterns permanently. Examples of flower essences include:

A) Walnut is used for transition or change
B) Honeysuckle is used for treating homesickness, grief and rescue animals
C) Apsen or Mimulus for treating irrational fears and anxiety

D) Crabapple for cleansing
E) Agrimony is used to improve communication between animals
F) Rock Rose helps restore calmness and courage
G) Beech improves the animal's tolerance for people and other animals

Other flower essence remedies include chestnut bud, chicory, cherry plum, clematis, gentian, heather, impatiens, larch, olive, vervain, vine, water violet, etc. You should seek advice from your local vet on the best remedy to use on your pet.

Touch Therapy

This is a bodywork technique that is used for healing, calming and training animals. Your pets can benefit from this type of therapy especially if done on a regular basis.

Touch therapy usually involves circular movements of the fingers and hands all over the animal's body. This is done to activate the cell function and awaken the cellular intelligence. The touch therapy method alters the nervous system, which thereby sends the messages to the brain. This enables the brain to engage damaged or rarely used parts of the body. Improvement of the animal's brain, together with the nervous system helps improve movement, behavior, mental status, and alleviates fear in the animals. With this kind of improvement, the animal's more aggressive behaviors are kept under control.

Touch areas usually include the mouth, ears, rump areas, as well as other parts of the animal's body. If done in the right manner, touch therapy can help speed up the healing of bad injuries, help cure diseases, and also help change any undesirable behaviors.

Touch therapy helps reduce lower back pain, cancer-related fatigue, blood pressure, post-operative pain, headache frequency, osteoarthritis of the knee, pain caused by cancer and symptoms of carpal tunnel syndrome.

The success of touch therapy on your pet depends on the qualifications of the veterinarian therapist. You need to find a certified therapist who can handle your pet with expertise. If you prefer to do it yourself, you may have to undergo an extensive training program so as to master the skills.

Applied Kinesiology

Applied kinesiology, also known as muscle strength testing, is a method of diagnosis and treatment, based on the belief that a number of muscles are linked to particular organs and glands, and that specific muscle weakness can be a sign of deeper internal problems such as reduced blood supply, nerve damage, chemical imbalances, and problems that organs and glands might be having.

Applied kinesiology is used to treat nervous system problems, energy imbalances in the body, nutritional deficiencies or excesses, and many other health problems.

How does Kinesiology work?

With Kinesiology, various types of muscles in the body are isolated after which pressure is applied to assess the strength of that individual muscle. This kind of muscle testing is used to assess whether there is any muscle stress that needs to be addressed. This is due to the fact that there are corresponding pairs muscles within the body and each pair may be having some typical imbalances that may affect it.

With Hair Testing, a sample of hair is assessed with the assistance of a surrogate. The weakness of the animal's energy can be assessed and remedies placed on the surrogate in order to strengthen the weakness in energy.

Applied Kinesiology helps solve a wide range of issues affecting the animal. They include behavioral problems, muscle and joint stiffness, performance problems, anxiety, injury-rehabilitation, hyper-sensitivity and many more.

It's important to look for a professional Kinesiologist who will be able to handle your pet with care and expertise.

Detox

A detox for your pet may be more beneficial to its health than you think. Just like in humans, detoxification involves removal of toxins and cleansing the body of other impurities to rebalance the system and restore health.

There are various reasons why you should consider a detox for your pets. Many chronic illnesses in today's cats, dogs and other pets are due to the heavy toxic load that they carry. Health conditions like ear infections, skin itching and irritation, diarrhea, vomiting and other complications might be a sign of toxin buildup. Pets are exposed to toxins from the environment and within the treats we buy them or from food we feed them off the table.

There are various natural detoxifiers available for your pet but should only be used as recommended by your local holistic vet.

Turmeric

The liver plays a major role in eliminating toxins from the body; in fact, the liver is at the heart of nearly ever biochemical process in the body. The body's ability to clot blood, breakdown harmful toxins, store energy and remove waste are all influenced by the liver and are impacted by liver health. The liver is a big player in your pet's digestion, storing vitamins and producing bile which breaks down fat. The curcumin in turmeric stimulates the bile production and thus fats are better absorbed and since a dog needs 20% fat in his/her diet this really boosts your dog's health. Turmeric boosts the body's ability to metabolize fat and get rid of waste and toxins.

Chlorella

This is a green food that is an excellent detoxifier. If using tablets, give one each day for a few days and then increase to two tablets for the other days and continue with the trend.

Garlic, astragalus and Echinacea all help support immune system function.

Cranberry, marshmallow, and corn silk help support kidney function.

Milk thistle helps detoxify the liver and stimulate regeneration of the liver cells.

Dandelion root, burdock root, Oregon grape, licorice, and other herbs help cleanse blood and improve liver function.

DAILY DOSAGE

Chlorella—If using tablets, give one each day for a few days and increase to 2 for another few days and so on.

Garlic—the suggested dose for cats and dogs is ½ a finely chopped raw clove mixed with food or ½ a capsule if using a supplement.

Cranberry—Dosage for cranberry capsules is given according to the weight of the pet.
Up to 11lbs-1/4 tablet each day,
12 lbs to 23 lbs-1/2 tablet each day,
24 lbs to 45 lbs-1 tablet each day, 46 lbs to
75 lbs-1 ½ tablets,
76 lbs to 90 lbs-2 tablets daily.

Astragalus—25mgs per 25 pounds

Echinacea—Best dosage is 1g/10kgs each day

Milk thistle—2mg for each lb. of the animal's weight

Marshmallow—½ tsp. per 10 lbs

Dandelion root—25ml of nonalcoholic tincture per 10 lbs

Apart from using herbs to detoxify your pets, exercise, diet, and water also play an important role in ensuring that the animal's body system is pure and well cleansed.

CHAPTER 4

DIET

HEMP and the benefits

Hemp is cannabis right? Should dogs be smoking weed?

There is far more to hemp than smoking pot, in fact it is a new super food that is being consumed by humans in seed form and as a non-dairy milk.

Hemp is indeed a variety of cannabis but it is also being safely used as a nutritious food supplement in the US and EU. Hemp dates back to 28th century BC. Since that time, it has proved extremely versatile and can be used for textiles and more importantly for oil.

You have heard many pet food brands boasting that they are filled with fish oils that are important for your pet's health – HEMP OIL is even better than fish oil as it has the perfect ratio of Omega 3 to Omega 6 fatty acids. Pets and humans cannot produce omega fatty acids and so they must be ingested via diet. As hemp oil is perfectly balanced it works synergistically with the body.

Hemp oil is also high in Gamma Linoleic Acid (GLA). GLA is a building block of enzymes called prostaglandins which are like hormones and which control inflammation, regulate body temperature and smooth muscle contractions.

GLA is great for:

CANCER

The American Cancer Society found a link between those who are low in GLA and the development of cancer, diabetes and skin allergies. Dogs suffer from these same ailments and so no doubt GLA can help them too. While dogs can make their own GLA, when they are stressed or doing a lot of exercise they may not be able to produce enough.

The British Journal of Cancer found that GLA is very effective in stopping brain and lung cancer.

GLA reduces inflammation and strengthens the immune system which are both vital in the fight against degenerative diseases.

JOINT PAIN REDUCTION

The Journal of Arthritis and Rheumatology found that the GLA found in hemp could reduce arthritic symptoms by 25%. It is indeed the perfectly balanced omega 3 and 6 which can naturally reduce inflammation.

SHINY COATS

Hemp has long been used in soaps and cosmetics as the oils are able to penetrate to the lower layers of the skin to nourish and encourage cell regeneration.

As the hemp reduces inflammation, it aids in combatting problems like pruritic skin disease, granulomas and dermatitis.

NOTE: Do not add hemp oil to food while cooking as it can become rancid which can lead to health problems for pets.
If your dog is on a chicken-based diet then flaxseed extract is a better option than hemp, as chicken is already rich in linoleic acid and it can cause an imbalance. (Ref: Steve Brown author of *Unlocking the Canine Ancestral Diet*.)
If your dog's diet is rich in meat and ruminants then hemp is a great supplement.

HOW MUCH HEMP

Steve Brown, mentioned above, recommends adding 1 teaspoon to 1- 1 ¼ pounds of food.

Does Your Pet Have a Food Intolerance?

NUTRISCAN

Is your pet unwell?
Does your pet suffer with severe digestive problems, anxiety, hypothyroidism, skin complaints or any other persistent ailment?

Have you thought about the fact that your pet may suffer food intolerances just like us humans increasingly do? NutriScan is a saliva-based food sensitivity and intolerance test for pets. You may find that your pet is allergic to cow's milk, soya, wheat, fish, peanuts, corn or a range of other foods which if removed from the diet can revolutionize their health.

NutriScan.org revealed that while food allergies that result in immediate and noticeable reactions are quite rare, food intolerances and sensitivities are far more common and can have a more subtle and yet increasingly severe effect over time. The reactions to food sensitivity and intolerance range across the board from chronic diarrhea and gastro intestinal problems to itchy flaky skin and hair loss.

NutriScan is quick and gives immediate results by testing the levels of IgA and IgM in the saliva. These antibodies are produced when your pet is reacting to a food intolerance and so they give a measure of any reactions taking place.

Does Your Pet Have Allergies?

Allergies, arthritis and other autoimmune diseases in humans and pets may be linked to a dysfunctional, or more commonly termed, 'leaky gut'.

What is a leaky gut? It sounds horrible, right?

Leaky guts occur when the gut's mucosal and semi-permeable intestinal lining is damaged. The purpose of the gut is to allow nutrients into the bloodstream and to stop undigested food, toxins and other undesirable materials from entering the body. However, with a leaky gut the intestine is more permeable and toxins along with other substances get through and cause a reaction.

As soon as the body detects these alien substances the immune system kicks in launching an 'attack' and the visible result is an outbreak of allergies. The more that leaks through, the greater the reaction.

But how does the gut get damaged in the first place?

There is a large amount of debate about this, but it boils down to an imbalance between the good and the bad bacteria in the gut. Antibiotics, vaccines, cortisone and other steroids, in addition to a highly processed diet, like kibble, are often at the root of the problem.
The bad bacteria and a yeast called Candida take over causing damaging inflammation and a leaky, dysfunctional gut.

So what do we do?

Avoid Kibble and antibiotics for one.

DIET

I guess it's a no-brainer that diet is key to a problem involving the gut, but every dog and cat is different and it is wisest to consult with

a holistic vet who is open-minded about nutritional therapy.
However, there are general rules to help alleviate the problem:
- Reduce your pets starch intake i.e. grains, potatoes and sweet potatoes
- No more sugary treats
- No chocolate or food from the table that is doused in sauces
- No bread or yeast

OMEGA 3's

Increase your pets' intake of these vital nutrients by adding hemp-based products, fish oils or chia seeds to their food.

PROBIOTICS

Probiotics can help give the good bacteria in the gut a boost. Try supplements, fermented goat's milk or kefir.
You can also try introducing pre-biotics – which are not actually probiotics but they encourage the development of probiotics. Pre-biotics can be found naturally in sprouted seeds.

ENZYMES

Digestive enzymes contained in whole raw foods can help break down food and are vital for tackling a leaky gut. Do your research well if you choose to use an enzyme in the form of a supplement.

GARLIC

Taken as suggested in the Flea Control Section, garlic repels the yeast which runs rampant when there is a leaky gut and can thus be effective in combatting this problem.

GLUTAMINE

This is an amino acid, naturally produced by the body, but when there is a leaky gut syndrome, which is causing stress, the levels of glutamine produced can drop. Glutamine fuels the cells that line the gut i.e., the mucosal cells, and is vital for restoring the gut and maintaining its efficacy. High protein foods like meat, fish and dairy are filled with glutamine.

HERBS

Calendula, slippery elm and chamomile are also helpful for a leaky gut.

CHAPTER 5

FLEAS – The Pet World's Biggest Bug Bear

Nontoxic Tick and Flea Control (Cats and Dogs)

Controlling ticks and fleas is a challenge when you want to do it naturally. Let's be honest, ticks and fleas have evolved over millennia and would probably be right out the hatch adapting and thriving even after a nuclear bomb.

There is increasing evidence that topical tick and flea treatments have increasingly severe side effects. The US Environmental Protection Agency (as reported on April 16, 2009) reported that it was redoubling the evaluation of spot-on pesticides and treatments for tick and flea control in pets due to an increase in the reported number of incidents involving adverse reactions from skin irritation to seizures and even death. The incidents reported involved shampoos, collars, sprays and spot-on treatments; however, the majority of incidents related to EPA-approved spot-on products.

If you analyse the life cycle of fleas (egg – larvae – pupae – adult) you will realize that while eggs make up 50% of the flea population, the irksome adults make up only 5%, with larvae and pupae somewhere in between. So from that you can see that if we target the eggs we have a shot at reducing the number of biting, irritating adults. Eggs are laid both on the pet and in other areas and they await ideal conditions to hatch. Larvae, the next phase, make up about 35% of the population: they feed off organic matter collecting in carpets, in cracks, on floors and in soil. The pupae are highly resistant to any form of control and they make up the remaining 10%.

So what do we do? We devise a way of zapping the eggs and the larvae. The mass market products which are often highly toxic are aimed mainly at the adults. The problem with these toxic products is that you have to be very careful; bugs and ticks become resistant to them, just as germs are now becoming resistant to antibiotics. Nature is resilient and the new generations of ticks and fleas come back stronger and ready to fight us. What is the answer? New, more toxic, more powerful chemicals? That cannot be the way going forward.

So what are the safer and more natural ways to rid your pet of these pesky fleas and ticks?

NEMATODES

These are for outdoor use.

Soil harbours flea larvae, so if your pet spends a few hours a day frolicking in the grass of your backyard you may want to give this a try. Nematodes are tiny worms, which can be applied via a spray can to your lawn. The nematodes prey on the flea larvae and can bring about a 90% reduction within a day.

Nematodes are totally safe, with the added benefit that they protect the garden from cutworm and grubs as well. Wet the soil before applying the nematodes and reapply periodically. Once the flea larvae have been eaten the nematode population will have nothing to eat and will die off.

BORIC ACID

If you have carpeting indoors then a boric acid treatment can eradicate the larvae section of the population without significant resistance building up and with no significant toxicity to pets or people. There are a number of boric acid products available and they may be labelled as carpet deodorizers or flea controllers. These products come as a fine power you sprinkle over the carpet; due to the fine particle size, it remains in the carpet after vacuuming. The powder kills the larvae effectively. While there are many products e.g., Fleago Natural Flea Control, apparently people also have success with 20 Mule Team Borax.

Shake powder (do don a mask as you don't want to breath the powder in) onto the carpet, rub or brush in, then vacuum. This should be good for a year, but do reapply if you shampoo or steam clean your carpets. I would recommend a good steam clean before the first application. Keep your pets away while you apply the borax.

NYLAR

If you have mainly stone, wood or laminate flooring then Nylar is a safe and effective product which you can use. Nylar mimics a juvenile hormone in the fleas, stopping them from becoming adults.

You can spray Nylar on floors, in kennels, on the dog's basket, etc. It regulates flea growth by preventing eggs from hatching and larvae from turning into adults. Again you need only apply once a year unless you clean the area with detergent, it is exposed to rain, or washed in a machine (e.g., dogs bedding).

It can be hard to find Nylar alone as it's often coupled with more toxic chemical ingredients in off-the-shelf products, so do read the label and use the Internet to find a Nylar product that is safe.

Treat each and every place your pet hangs out with Nylar or Borate and do not neglect cracks behind sofa cushions and hard to reach places. If your cat or dog likes to get into bed with you, normal detergent and washing and drying should eliminate eggs and larvae from bed linen.

But my pet already has fleas.

As long as you are patient, a flea comb can work very well, but it takes up to a month to work, as the adults last many weeks and the pupae present may still hatch. Use the flea comb to comb out the hair all over your pet at least once a day and dip it in warm soap water to kill the fleas.

Lather kills fleas as well and so a bath with any natural product that works up a good lather can kill the fleas. Bathing alone will not control the fleas and can be very drying on the pets' skin and of course is no good for cats. However, bathing is a quick solution and if you add some essential oils (e.g., lavender, citronella, pennyroyal, eucalyptus), you can further repel fleas from hopping aboard your pooch for a ride. Again DO NOT use essential oils for CATS as they tend to be too sensitive to them.

As shampoos go: Johnson's Baby Shampoo and Head and Shoulders appear to be popular.

FLEA ZAPPERS

A flea zapper is an inexpensive electronic comb which kills 3-4 fleas on one action and is totally chemical free, as it work via a voltage which is harmless to dogs, cats, kittens, puppies and elderly pets.

It should NOT be used by pet owners who have epilepsy or a heart condition. By all means, get one and get your kids or partner to do the zapping for you.

FLEA TRAPS

You can use these to attract and kill fleas from 25 meters away 24 hours a day. Chemical free and totally safe to use. A trap can hold up to 10,000 fleas and it is almost unbreakable.

The Spring Star Flea Trap seems to be the best on the market.

I think this works well with dogs who are often taken to public places where they pick up more fleas – take your dogs to a room i.e. garage where the flea trap is switched on and leave them there for a while when they get home so to destroy any new fleas they may have picked up.

CEDAR OIL

This works well on ticks, fleas and bed bugs and is entirely safe for mammals. Cedar oil interrupts the pheromones which are the means by which the bugs communicate with each other and find food. Look for a natural organic product range which sells cedar oil.

Evolv contains cedar oil and is great for pets that have fleas and ticks already (as it kills them) or when you are taking your dogs into a flea infested area and need a repellent. If you use it on your cat proceed with care as cats are often highly sensitive to essential oils – try a small area near the shoulders and see how your cat gets on. Stop use immediately if your cat begins to vomit or experience discomfort within 12 hours and wash the cedar oil off with mild soapy water. If your cat fares well, try a larger area the next day.

GARLIC and YEAST

While it is true that feeding these to your pet boosts their nutrition level and makes them less tasty to ticks and fleas, it should not ever be your only line of defence against the tick and flea army.

For cats, try 1 teaspoon of yeast flakes (make sure they are the ones for nutritional purposes, not baking) and one small clove of garlic.

For bigger dogs use ¼ cup of yeast and 2 3 large cloves of garlic.

NOTE: Large doses of garlic (or indeed onions) can cause anaemia in dogs and cats.

FLEA PILLS

Since this book is all about natural health products, I will not be recommending these. Dogs, cats and humans are already ingesting way too many chemicals that our bodies are just not equipped to deal with in terms of the fact that we cannot detoxify from these substances. There are no real indicators of the harm long-term use can do, even though trials suggest short-term use is safe.

CONCLUSION

You should now have many more options to deal with ticks and fleas safely and remember that the more healthy and well-nourished you dogs and cats are, the less likely they are to attract fleas and ticks as these bugs chose the weaker animals.

CHAPTER 6

Long- and Short-Term Ailments and How to Treat Them

If you really care about your pets' health and wellness, then it's important to be aware of the long-term and short-term illnesses and conditions that they are prone to. Some conditions might need to be treated by a vet for a short time and others may go on for a long period of time, even for life.

With the alternative medicine, short-term and long-term illnesses can be fully treated and recurrence of such ailments prevented. Below is a list of different ailments; long-term and short-term and how they can be treated.

Short-Term Ailments in Pets and How to Treat Them

Gastrointestinal Disorders and Digestive Problems

Gastrointestinal problems affect the animal's stomach and intestines and this results in great pain and other problems. Some of the most common signs that your pet is suffering from gastrointestinal problems include vomiting, diarrhoea, flatulence, weakness, constipation, and regurgitation. Apart from using different nutritional approaches to help increase the healing process, alternative medicine can be used to not only treat the ailment, but to address the root of the problem.

Ginger is excellent for nausea or vomiting affecting your dog. Nausea may be caused by travel sickness or cancer treatments. Use fresh ginger (a small amount) or the powdered version 30 minutes before the dog takes a car trip.
Ginger is also very useful for bloating – gastric dilation volvulus is a life threatening condition which affects mainly the larger breeds of

dog. Ginger stimulates movement within the stomach and accelerates stomach emptying and in this way can prevent and relieve gastric bloating.

Herbal medicine like peppermint oil, arnica, slippery elm bark and many more are usually very effective for gastrointestinal problems. These herbs include:

- Licorice - This is a powerful anti-inflammatory, anti-allergenic, anti-viral and an excellent tonic for the intestines, bladder, kidney, and the entire digestive tract. It also helps in the treatment of peptic ulcers and promotes the healing of the stomach lining.

- Slippery Elm - Is an excellent digestive herb that is rich in trace minerals, manganese, protein, iodine, and soothing mucilage. It's regularly used to treat chronic, as well as acute, digestive disorders.

- Marshmallow - Is a well-known remedy for digestive disorders, and highly effective in soothing painful mucus membranes of the digestive tract.

NOTE: It's always advisable to seek advice from a professional holistic pet practitioner to avoid any complications especially from using these herbs in the wrong dosages.

External and Internal Injuries

Aloe Vera is used for skin irritations, minor burns, sunburns, or skin inflammations. It should be applied gently on the affected part with the fingers.

Arnica gel is topically used to treat bruises, sore muscles and joints, and sprains.

Turmeric – This is a powerful anti-inflammatory, antiseptic and antibiotic due to its active ingredient curcumin. It can be used to cleanse wounds and keep infection at bay. Mix with honey to make a topical paste that can be easily applied. Of course, honey has antibacterial properties as well. Do cover the areas, as honey tastes nice and may attract flies, or get licked off.

Chest Problems

Pets also experience chest congestion as well as dry and bronchial coughs which can be treated by use of a herb known as mullein. The herb is used for its antiseptic and mild analgesic properties. It is used for whooping cough, coughs, bronchitis, pneumonia, colds, flu, chills, sore throats and other ailments. The best way to get results is to have your pet ingest the mullein leaves.

Acupuncture is also effective in this case at it helps relieve chest congestion.

Cold Problems

As with humans, colds require urgent treatment before the lungs are affected. Although this is usually a short-term illness, it should be treated effectively. Your pet may occasionally suffer common colds, influenza, or even sore throats. Several natural remedies can be used to treat these ailments.

Herbal supplements in this case are very effective in fighting off infections. Garlic is an excellent microbial that kills bacteria and viruses caused by common cold viruses. Lemon, turmeric, and other herbal teas also work well to treat colds in pets.

Dental Diseases

Periodontal Disease is a disease caused by the accumulation of tartar on the surface of the pets' teeth or on the gum line, which eventually leads to teeth destruction. Some of the most common signs to look out for include discoloured teeth, reddened gums, reluctance to eat, drooling, and swelling of the face. There are several natural remedies that can be used to help treat the disease and prevent further progression. Since the disease also causes bad breath, there are various herbs such as green tea, mint leaves, and others that can be used to get rid of it.

Dental diseases in pets may deprive them of the joy of a good bone or pig's ear, and even lead to severe weight loss. If your pet is suffering from periodontal disease, it may result in nauseating halitosis and what's more, the inflammation in their mouths can lead to a spread of bacteria into their bloodstream and onto the internal organs. The bacteria can harm the heart, kidney, liver and other internal body organs. Fish oils like Nordic Naturals will help reduce any gum inflammation. Strong organic green or black tea or dry tea leaves rubbed on the gum between the teeth may help stop plaque accumulation.

Obesity and dental problems in pets are inextricable linked to highly processed foods, especially those high in cereals. Foods packed with simple carbohydrates and sugars provide nourishment for the oral bacteria that can be rapidly absorbed. Commercial pet foods contain up to 40% of sugars and carbos and so it's obvious how they contribute to this problem.

Again the raw food pet diet (see chapter 8) can help eliminate this problem and the raft of related issues e.g., kidney, liver, heart and fertility issues.

First Aid – the Herbal Way

Would you like to put together a doggie and kitty first aid kit made from nothing but herbs?

You are about to learn how.

While herbs are accessible, cost effective and potent they also support your dog's long terms health as they have antibacterial, antifungal and antiseptic properties with none of the immune suppressing ingredients many regular first aid kits have, which can damage long term health.

So what problems is our herbal health kit going to address?

* Cuts and bruises
* Rashes
* Scrapes
* Insect bites
* Muscle pain and aches
* Burns
* Abscesses
* Bleeding

Which herbs are up to the job?

Calendula

Calendula helps heal skin quickly by helping to regenerate the skin, it can even prevent scarring. What's more, it is antifungal, antibacterial and anti-viral, which helps the wound to stay infection free.

Calendula is ideal for cuts, burns, abscesses, scrapes, bites and fungal infections and can be applied as a salve or tea. Take care when applying calendula to an infected wound as the calendula causes wounds and abscesses to heal so fast that the skin may actually seal the infection in – thus you must make sure the wound is not draining before you use the calendula.

Comfrey

Comfrey has a reputation for healing body tissue fast and that includes muscles, tendons and bones, not only skin.

You can apply the comfrey topically as a salve, poultice or tea and it will speed up the healing process for sore muscles, burns and swelling. Dried comfrey can be used to stop bleeding: you can apply the dried herb directly to the skin. Keep it handy when cutting your pet's nails.

Plantain

There is nothing fancy about plantain; in fact, it is a weed found all over North America, usually besides the road. Plantain is a fantastic anti-inflammatory and can be used to effectively treat bites, stings, burns, bug bites and poison ivy. It is also highly effective when used to draw thorns or other foreign bodies from paws or ears.
Use as a poultice and apply directly to the affected area.
To make the poultice: crush or mash up some leaves and apply to the skin.

Aloe (Barbadenis)

Aloe is known for its ability to sooth. Many of you may already use it to treat burns in humans. It can be grown as a potted plant and you simply break of a piece to release the soothing gel. It is very easy to grow indoors or outside.
When applied to a burn right away it both soothes, relieves pain and irritation and helps kick-start the healing process.
In non-burn wounds it promotes soft tissue healing and increases the blood supply.

Freshly cut aloe works best as bacteria tends to spread in the off the counter aloe juice and gels. Do not use on severs burns, deep wounds or infected wounds.

Yarrow

Also called Bloodwort, Old Man's Pepper, Milfoil and Thousand Weed, yarrow is a commonplace weed that grows almost everywhere in gardens, meadows and alongside roads. You can make use of the fresh leaves, the salve or a poultice.

Yarrow works as an anti-inflammatory and also helps stop bleeding and aids the building of new tissue. It works well as a poultice on bruises and strains. It is also effective used as a tea on bites, cuts, burns and stings as it has great antifungal and antibacterial properties.

So what is a salve and how do I make one?

Salves are like balms and are very easy to make at home. Here are some standard ingredients:

8-10 oz of the relevant herb
2-3 Cups of Coconut Oil
1 oz Beeswax

You can use one or more herbs in the salve mixture. Always use organic herbs and try to buy them ground. The finer they are ground the more they release their healing properties. Alternatively, grind the herbs yourself in a coffee grinder.

Place the herbs and the coconut oil into a double boiler or slow cooker and set to very low and allow to warm for a day or two. When the oil takes on the colour of the herb you can be sure that the magical qualities of the herb have transferred to the oil. Once this has happened strain the oil through a few layers of cheese cloth to remove all the grit from the herbs. Now mix in 1 oz of beeswax for every 8 oz of herbal oil. Place the beeswax back into the crockpot and allow to melt into the oil slowly. Remove from heat and pour into a wide-mouthed jar. Store at room temperature.

How do you make a topical herbal tea?

Use 4 tablespoons of organic dried herbs or 8 tablespoons of fresh herbs and place into a dark coloured teapot. Add 2 cups of boiling water. Allow to seep for at least 20-25 minutes, then drain. Allow to cool.
The best way to use the tea is to place it once cooled into a spray bottle and use it to spritz the affected area 3-4 times a day.

Witch Hazel

You may already have this in your medicine cabinet to use as an astringent. Use on a cotton pad and apply to cuts, grazes, bug bites and stings.

Helichrysum

This is part of the sunflower family. Helichrysum italicum is used to make a yellow-reddish essential oil.

Mix 1 drop of lavender essential oil and one drop of helichrysum essential oil with 1 teaspoon of aloe vera gel and a ½ teaspoon of green clay. Then add witch hazel gradually until a nice paste develops.
Apply to wasp sting welts.
DO NOT USE ON CATS.

How can herbs and aromatherapy help pets who suffer with allergies?

Hydrosols are the best way to help your pets experience the benefits of aromatherapy when they are suffering from seasonal allergies. Hydrosols have all the great properties of essential oils but are less concentrated and thus gentler for pets who may already be hypersensitive to smells during allergy season.
You can even make ice cubes from hydrosols which can be used on bug bites or welts to soothe and reduce inflammation and irritation.

The ideas below are for dogs and horses, NOT cats.

Bathing: During allergy season bath your dog at least once a week to make sure the excess pollens and grass seeds are washed from their coats. When your dogs is itching and scratching their coats get greasier and adhere to more allergens, which is another reason a good bath is a great thing.

A foot spa: Grass pollens may cause itchy red and swollen paws. Have a plastic tub of clean lukewarm water ready and bathe off the feet of your pooch ensuring the areas between the paw pads are flushed out as grass pollens can accumulate there. Dry with a soft cotton cloth and be gentle.

Dry Cleaning: Wiping your dog down with a wet cotton cloth can help remove excess pollens between bath times. Wipe his face, body and legs. Keep a separate cloth for each dog and when you wash these clothes use a non-bio, non-scented laundry detergent and dry inside or on the dryer rather than on the wash line where they just attract more pollens.

A soothing bath time blend for you dog

In a glass jar or bottle mix:

1 cup distilled water
¼ cup lavender hydrosol
25-30ml or 2 tablespoons pure liquid soap

Mix together ingredients. After dousing your dog in warm water, lather this blend into his coat and massage with love. Rinse off well and follow with an apple cider vinegar rinse.

Apple Cider Vinegar Rinse

This rinse can soothe itchy skin, calm rashes and welts; and what's more, it aids natural skin recovery by restoring the skin's normal ph. This rinse will also keep fleas, biting flies and gnats at bay. Allow the rinse to dry on the dogs coat for the added benefit of bug relief.

½ cup apple cider vinegar
½ cup green tea (already made)
1 cup distilled water

This keeps for one week to ten days in the fridge and can be used as a spritz for topical bug treatments.

Long-Term Ailments in Pets and How to Treat Them

Keeping yourself informed about your pets' illnesses and symptoms is important to keep them safe. Apart from short-term illnesses that can be treated easily, pets also suffer from chronic illnesses which can cause severe health problems or even cause death. Here are some of the major long-term illnesses affecting pets.

Arthritis and Joint Pain

As it is with human beings, animals too are affected by arthritis. Arthritis occurs when there are abnormal changes in the joints. Some of the most common symptoms associated with arthritis especially with dogs are lameness, stiffness, slowed movement and pain. While there might not be any cure for arthritis, there are various herbal supplements like omega oils, vitamins, and holistic treatments such as acupuncture and chiropractic, which may help keep your pet as mobile as possible.

Clinical studies have shown that the curcumin in turmeric has a powerful antioxidant effect on the free radicals that cause painful inflammation and damage to joints affected by arthritis. Organic turmeric added to your pets food can help alleviate arthritis in dogs and horses quite dramatically. Turmeric is also a pain reliever which can benefit you dog and horse if they suffer from arthritis.

Ginger, an anti-inflammatory, is also useful in the fight against arthritis.

Dogs with arthritis may respond to natural remedies without experiencing any possible side effects. There is a plant-based formula that was created by a University of Montreal Professor in two stages.
The first stage consisted of devil's claws, curcumin, pineapple bromelaine, chamomile, willow bark, black current, and Salai (Indian frankincense). The second stage involved adding roster supplements such as omega 3, glutamine, and chondroitin sulphate.

This formula was created to help treat the inflammation that is associated with arthritis in dogs. The additional supplements were meant to help promote healing of the joints.

Diet is a very important factor when it comes to arthritis. Feeding your pets a good diet that is rich in various nutrients can give dramatic improvements. All foods must be organic and prepared under extremely hygienic conditions. It's good to identify foods that may cause allergies because they may increase joint inflammations. Essential oils also help reduce inflammation and reduce joint pains.

Another key factor in alleviating arthritis is controlling weight. Being overweight not only makes the disease accelerate but also causes a lot of pain. Regular exercise is very important.

Maintaining a healthy gastrointestinal system goes a long way toward preventing further inflammations.

Acupuncture is extremely helpful for pets with various arthritic conditions. Chiropractic adjustments and massages contort the spine when trying to move in such a way that it helps minimize joint pain.

Other than that, arthritis can be managed with proper diet, especially one that helps cleanse the body by removing harmful toxins. Exercise should also be incorporated to help strengthen the joints.

Cancer

Animals develop cancer, just like humans. The good news is that there are alternate cancer treatments for pets. Yes, cancer in pets can be treated by use of traditional remedies.

Traditional veterinary cancer treatments are very effective and readily available. Herbal medicine and supplements are also used to treat cancer and reduce the pain. There are two herbal supplements under research that are believed to have cancer-fighting abilities. They include curcumin and artemisinin.

You heard me talk of curcumin before – it is the active ingredient in turmeric. A recent study at UCLA found that turmeric blocks the cancer promoting enzyme which stimulates head and neck cancer. The Department of Small Animal Clinical Scientists discovered during their studies that curcumin inhibited tumor growth and could even shrink tumours thanks to its uncanny ability to restrict, or even shut down, the blood vessels feeding tumours.

Turmeric has antioxidant properties which also help alleviate the negative impact of chemotherapy.

How do you administer turmeric to your pet?

Dosage is approximately 15-20 mg per pound of body weight in dogs or 150-200 mg for cats. Alternatively, Use 1/8 to 1/4 teaspoon a day for every 10lbs of dog weight. Make sure your pet is fully hydrated and not constipated. Sprinkle organic turmeric powder, or the root (which looks a little like ginger) peeled and crushed mixed into your pet's food. If you cook your pet's food from scratch add it into the recipe. Supermarket turmeric may have low potency or contain chemicals, so use organic turmeric from a reputable supplier and store in a cool dry place. Turmeric is absorbed better when mixed with a small amount of black pepper and fish oil.

Artemisinin is an extract from wormwood and hails from Chinese medicine. Seattle scientists have found that it is highly effective at killing human breast cancer cells. Dr. Henry Lai, a bioengineering researcher at the University of Washington, Seattle also discovered that a pet dog who could not even walk across the room as its osteosarcoma was so severe, made a complete recovery after only 5 days and was still alive two years later. All thanks to artemisinin, which is highly effective and selective, and proving toxic to cancer cells and harmless to normal cells.

Artemix is a good choice as it contains artemisinin, artesunate and artemether, is readily available, and can be taken orally by your pet. It is best to avoid iron rich food, e.g., red meat, 3-4 hours before giving Artemix. And again, keep your pet fully hydrated and well exercised. The dose is determined as 1 milligram of artemether per kg of body weight per day, preferably given with butyrate and vitamin D-3. Your pet should not have had radiotherapy for two months prior to this treatment. Seek advice from a pet health expert for your peace of mind.

Inflammation plays a role in cancer development and proliferation so using ginger as a nutrient can support in the fight against this disease as it has anti-inflammatory properties and it boosts the immune system.

Apart from the use of herbal supplements to help fight cancer, there are various homeopathic therapies used to help fight cancer in pets. They include:

Antioxidant Therapy - Include dietary antioxidants which help improve immune function, decrease toxicity to non-cancerous cells, increase tumour response to chemo and radiation therapy, and help reverse metabolical changes.

Poly-MVA Therapy - Therapy works by introducing synthetic mimics of electric pathways in which cancer cells are destroyed.

Ozone Therapy - In this therapy, anaerobic life forms that cause cancer are immersed in an IV fluid for a certain period of time to extinguish cancer causing microbes.

Diabetes

Common signs of diabetes in pets (like dogs) include frequent urination, thirst, rapid weight loss, loss of appetite or abdominal pain.

This is a common disease in middle aged and older cats and dogs, but it can affect pets of any age. Being overweight or suffering from an inflamed pancreas can make a pet predisposed to this disease. Glucocorticoids and cortisone type drugs which are often used for heat control may actually cause diabetes. Putting your pet on a weight loss diet and never feeding them scraps from the table is the best way to prevent this disease in the first place. In addition, fresh food, raw food, species appropriate food and the avoidance of all unnecessary vaccines can help your pet avoid diabetes. Anecdotal evidence suggests pets fed a totally raw diet never develop diabetes. At the very least reduce processed food and increase your pet's intake of fresh natural ingredients.

Use of alternative medicine can help treat diabetes and reduce the pain associated with the disease. Apart from dietary supplements and herbs, holistic treatment is often very useful. Acupuncture provides an excellent supportive treatment for animals with diabetes.

Good quality supplements are also recommended so as to improve the animal's immune system. This is important because many diabetic animals have a weakened immune system. Multi-vitamin and mineral supplements are very important in this case.

Essential Fatty Acids have been shown to enhance glucose metabolism and also help protect against cardiovascular problems in diabetes.

If managed properly, diabetes may not necessarily make the animals life unbearable. There are still many animals living happy and healthy lives.

Liver and Kidney Diseases

These types of diseases can be fatal if not detected early. Being an attentive pet owner and recognizing these symptoms early can help quicken the treatment process. There are various herbs and homeopathic treatments that can be used to increase the chances of recovery.

Other long-term illnesses that can be treated by use of alternative medicine include heart diseases, urinary illnesses, and other serious illness. A good diet can also go a long way in promoting healing in pets suffering from long-term illnesses.

Heartworm

Conventional treatment for heartworm is both difficult and risky as these treatments are packed with chemicals.
In a recent study, ginger was shown to have great potential for treating heartworm. The reduction in the microfilarial concentration was as high as 83-98% in infected dogs treated with ginger. This means that heartworm larvae suffered a dramatic fall off thanks to the ginger.

Study http://www.ncbi.nlm.nih.gov/pubmed/3668217

Cushing Disease

Cushing Disease is a serious disease affecting middle-aged dogs and horses.

While the most obvious sign is hair loss and patches of baldness other common signs include increased thirst and urination, skin infections, pot-bellied appearance, increased panting, and increased appetite. This condition develops when the adrenal glands secrete huge amounts of steroid hormones such as cortisol. Cushing disease tends to be over diagnosed and often the symptoms coincide with that of general aging, so you have to take care before rushing to judgment. Make sure you investigate thoroughly with your vet and have the thyroid of your dog or horse tested as well to make sure it is not a thyroid issue rather than Cushing.

If your pet is negative for Cushing but still experiences hair loss then try Homeopathic Formic Acid to restore a patchy, shabby coat to its former glory.

If it is a thyroid problem rather than Cushing then use Homeopathic Thyroid 30c at one drop a day for 3 weeks to restore the thyroid to normal.

Cushing Disease results from excess production of a hormone from the outer part of the adrenal gland a result of either:

1)   A tumour on the adrenal gland or
2)   A benign tumour on the pituitary gland which stimulates the adrenal gland.

Since the pituitary gland is the ringmaster, in terms of the endocrine system and it controls hormones which in turn influence the endocrine glands, a tumour in the pituitary gland can cause excess corticosteroid to be produced which results in hair loss. Other symptoms are sweating, weight-loss, listlessness and anaemia.

Homeopathic remedies are useful when the disease is detected early.

Homeopathic Pituitary – This remedy is actually made from the posterior lobe of the pituitary gland and it can aid in the re-balancing of the gland. It is given in low potency doses over a long period of time with monitoring of progress.

Homeopathic Formic Acid – If administered in the early stages this can be very effective. This is administered over a 1-2 month period. It not only restores the coat but the overall health of the pet.

Herbs and supplements like rosehips, nettle, wormwood, clivers, clover, nettle, kelp, milk thistle and apple cider vinegar can be given as tinctures to aid the treatment of Cushing Disease but this should be done in conjunction with your holistic vet who can recommend combinations and dosages.

If your pet is on cortisone and you wish to take him off to try homeopathic remedies, make sure to consult with a reputable homeopathic vet first.

Cognitive Dysfunction

Cognitive Dysfunction is also a major chronic illness in pets. Also known as dementia, the disease basically progresses with age and may also be caused by the depletion of dopamine in the brain. Some of the most common symptoms include urinary accidents, confusion, anxiety, pacing, and trouble remembering the family members.

Herbs, diet and natural supplements can help prevent and alleviate symptoms of the disease.

Pancreatitis

Pancreatitis is a common ailment in dogs and cats. The disease is caused by inflammation of the pancreas which further leads to intra-abdominal leakage of the digestive enzymes. Common signs and symptoms are vomiting, lack of appetite, jaundice, lethargy, and abdominal pain. If left untreated for a long period of time, pancreatitis can cause severe organ damage or even worse, brain damage.

The disease can be controlled by providing a well-balanced diet and should only contain organic foods. Essential fatty acid supplements are also essential as well as multivitamins. Use of certain herbs can also help detoxify, cleanse, and nourish the pet's body. Acupuncture and chiropractic treatments are also important to help treat tight back muscles.

CHAPTER 7

How to Approach Supplements and Natural Foods for Your Pet. They Are What They Eat!

Is your pet having signs and symptoms of nutritional deficiency? Then it means that he's not getting enough key nutrients in his diet. Nutrition is the main foundation of good health in our pets and diet is the most important component for your pet's overall health. Just like your diet, your pet's diet must include all the required foods to maintain a healthy body and boost their immune system.

There are many chronic illnesses affecting our pets due to lack of proper nutrients in their diets. Most of these ailments revolve around the breaking down of the pets' immune system. These diseases have been triggered by use of commercial pet foods that contain toxic chemicals. Have you ever wondered why so many people are turning to natural foods today? It's because they have realized that they are essential in building stronger bodies and helping to prolong life. The same case applies to our pets. This means that treating them with alternative medicine is not enough. They need to be fed with organic foods to eliminate the chances of contracting diseases triggered by nutritional deficiencies.

There are various ways to ensure that your pet stays in good health, e.g. using dietary supplements and natural foods instead of feeding your pet commercially prepared foods that contain harmful ingredients.

Before you decide about giving dietary supplements and natural food to your pets, there are a few considerations that you must take into account. One of them is the pet's health. If your pet is suffering from ailments such as arthritis, skeletal problems, hair loss, immune system problems, digestive problems or even nutritional deficiencies, then you must include dietary supplements to boost health. Also, age of the pet is another thing to take into account because aging dogs and cats have poor health and lack energy to even play around. These supplements help improve health, boost the immune system, and increase energy in the body.

Dietary Supplements

There are various supplements that are highly recommended by vets because they can greatly benefit the health of your pet.

Multi-Vitamin Dietary Supplement - Multi-vitamin supplements are some of the most proven and effective. They are 100% safe natural supplements that have the most appropriate ingredients needed to promote a pet's overall health. Vitamin supplements help support brain, liver, kidney, heart and eye functions. They contain useful minerals and antioxidants which help give the pet's coat a shinier, smoother coat, and improve overall health.

These supplements benefit the pets in a number of ways. One, they help increase the body's energy levels since they promote overall well-being of your pet. Secondly, they help strengthen the immune system, thereby helping prevent disease infections.

Calcium Supplements are also important for bone formation, muscle contraction, blood coagulation, and nerve impulse transmission.

Oil and Fat Supplements (e.g., fish oil, hemp) help promote overall growth, body tissue maintenance and increase energy.

Choosing the Right Supplements

The most commonly used natural dietary supplements products for pets are those used to strengthen the joints, improve the digestive system, protect and condition the skin and hair coat.

Before buying these natural supplements for your pets, there are a few things that you should consider for safety purposes. Always check the product quality, efficacy, tolerance (some may cause allergic reactions), and safety (have they been clinically tested).

The overall function of all types of supplements is to:

- Increase overall body health
- Increase energy
- Increase vitality
- Improve the immune system
- Improve overall cell health
- Promote the body's natural ability to get rid of toxins
- Help improve normal brain function
- Improve body's physical function

However, as much as we would love to promote our pets' health by use of dietary supplements, there are health risks involved. Some may cause liver damage and lower kidney function. It's always good to proceed cautiously when using supplements for safety. If the pet shows any undesirable symptoms when the supplements are given, it's good to seek a vet's advice before proceeding. All in all, positive effects outnumber the negative ones.

All in all, dietary supplements are a good health choice for pets and must be incorporated on a daily basis to promote their overall health.

Benefits of Feeding Your Pet with Natural Foods

Feeding your pet with an organic or all-natural diet with natural pet food can help improve their overall health, boost immunity and improve overall appearance. The most surprising thing is that more and more pet food companies sell organic and natural pet foods these days.

Natural foods blend nature's finest and most digestible foods such as whole foods, digestible proteins, a complete blend of vitamins, minerals, and Omega fatty acids.

Apart from packed pet foods, you can also consider feeding them with raw foods so as to gain maximum benefits. Raw food is essential not only for promoting growth and health, but also in strengthening their teeth. These raw foods include beef, chicken, fish, vegetables, and other naturally occurring foods that are recommended for pets.

Natural foods have numerous health benefits to the pets. These benefits include:

Promote Overall Health and Strong Immunity - Organic foods provide better nutritional substances that help promote overall health and also boost the immune system, thus making it easier for the pets to fight diseases and infections.

Improves Life Quality and Longevity - Natural foods have a positive impact on your pets and thus, they are able to live a healthier and happy life.

Helps Reduce Digestive Disorders - Lack of chemicals and other artificial substances in natural foods helps improve food digestion and improve overall well-being of the digestive system.

Reduction of Skin Ailments and Allergies - Foods containing harsh chemicals as preservatives may cause severe allergic reactions. With natural foods, it's very rare for a pet to suffer from allergic reactions since they contain no preservatives or chemicals.

Healthier Skin and Coat - A natural diet contains all useful nutrients needed for growth and overall appearance. Fruits and vegetables contain essential vitamins that help promote healthy skin and coat.

Better Weight Management - Many of the commercial pet foods on the market today contain dangerous additives and chemicals that increase the pet's body weight. It's not unusual to find some dogs and cats suffering from obesity. Natural foods contain no additives that may increase the animal's weight and thus, it's a much healthier option.

Raw Food Diet

You may have heard of the raw food diet for humans, but I mentioned earlier that pets on the raw food diet do not develop diabetes and are less prone to other diseases. But what is the raw food diet for pets all about?

You may be concerned that your dog will not get enough nutrition with an exclusively raw menu. I am sure that many of you already incorporate vegetables into your pets' diet for added vitamins and minerals, but you may fear that carnivorous dogs should not be eating that many veggies. What follows is a guide to the mineral and vitamin content of many foodstuffs which you can incorporate into your pets' diet.

There are many nutritionally rich foods which you can add to your dog's diet to give him a boost of vitamins without having to mince up the veggies. Natural food stuffs, rather than their synthetic substitutes are always the safest source of vitamin and minerals and many herbs provide essential nutrients along with co factors needed to boost your pet's short- and long-term health. Feeding your dog a wide range of veg and plant based ingredients can boost immune function, slow aging, prevent eye problems and skin irritations as well as supporting tooth and bone formation.

VITAMIN 101

VITAMIN A

Essential for immune system, helps maintain good eyesight, strengthens skin and also protects against colds and infection. It is a powerful antioxidant.

Meat sources: pork, eggs, salmon, sardines, liver, kidney, brain and chicken.

Vegetable sources: watercress, yellow dock, chickweed, fennel seed, hops, kelp, lemongrass, horsetail, rose hips, sage, parsley, mullein, nettle, burdock root and red clover.

VITAMIN B1 (Thiamine)

Promotes growth, improves mental functioning, nourishes the immune system helping combat stress and it also aids digestion.

Meat sources: liver, rabbit, chicken, turkey, lamb, goat, buffalo, beef, halibut and haddock.

Vegetable sources: alfalfa, fenugreek, nettle, chamomile, yarrow, yellow dock, catnip, oat straw, chickweed, eye bright.

VITAMIN B2 (Riboflavin)

Essential for red blood cell formation. It also promotes a great coat of hair and healthy skin. Important for growth and reproduction.

Meat sources: liver, heart, chicken, goat, lamb, turkey, ostrich, egg, beef, pork and rabbit.

Vegetable sources: catnip, sage, fennel seed, ginseng, horsetail, nettle, bladder wrack, cayenne and raspberry leaves.

VITAMIN B3 (Niacin)

This vitamin is vital for good circulation and healthy skin. B3 is an energy vitamin - improving vitality and aiding digestion.

Meat sources: rabbit, tuna, sardine, lamb, goat, turkey, pork, chicken and salmon.

Vegetable sources: alfalfa, slippery elm, licorice, nettle, peppermint, red clover, chickweed, mullein and rose hips.

VITAMIN B5 (Pantothenic Acid)

This vitamin is essential for a healthy immune system, for wound healing and fighting infection. It also helps prevent anaemia and improves stamina and strength.

Meat sources: liver, kidney, heart, turkey, goat, lamb, beef, halibut, haddock and sardine.

Vegetable sources: alfalfa, burdock root, nettle and yellow dock.

VITAMIN B6 (Pyridoxine)

B6 is another digestion vitamin, as it is need to produce hydrochloric acid. This aids in digestion of fats, e.g., omega 3, 6 and 9, which are the fundamental building block hormones as well as proteins. B6 also helps prevent kidney stones which are often a problem for pets. This vitamin can reduce allergic reactions and it helps treat arthritis.

Meat sources: eggs, beef, rabbit, turkey, goat, ostrich, chicken, liver, heart, salmon, halibut and sardines

Vegetable sources: catnip, oat straw and alfalfa.

VITAMINS B8 (Folate, Folic Acid)

Meat sources: beef, liver, rabbit, turkey, goat, lamb, ostrich, haddock, sardine, halibut and pork.

Vegetable sources: rosemary, dandelion, parsley, spirulina.

VITAMIN B12 (Cyanocobalamin)

Improves mental function and concentration, and helps combat anaemia and aids digestion.

Meat sources: kidney, liver, sardines, buffalo, rabbit, turkey, pork and goat.

Vegetable sources: alfalfa, bladderwrack and hops.

VITAMIN C (Ascorbic Acid)

This aids the absorption of iron and calcium and we all know that Vitamin C is key to warding off colds, flu and even cancer, as it supports the immune system. It is also a powerful antioxidant which is vital for tissue repair and functioning and adrenal gland function.

Meat sources: liver, heart, kidney and fish.

Vegetable sources: skullcap, violet leaves, kelp, horsetail, oat straw, parsley, chickweed, alfalfa, fennel seeds, fenugreek, red clover, nettle and hops.

VITAMIN D

Your body cannot metabolise calcium and phosphorus without Vitamin D, thus this is vital for bone and teeth health. Vitamin D plays a role in heartbeat regulation and can help reduce chances of cancer by enhancing immunity. It also plays a role in blood clotting and thyroid function.

Meat sources: egg, sardine, liver, kidney, tuna.

Vegetable sources: alfalfa, horsetail, nettle and parsley.

VITAMIN E

Another antioxidant which guards against cancer and heart disease by preventing cell damage. It also, as most of you know, promotes healthy skin and hair, while reducing blood pressure.

Meat sources: ostrich, buffalo, egg, halibut, haddock, sardines, kidney, liver and brain.

Vegetable sources: bladderwrack, dandelion, flaxseed, raspberry leaf, rose hips, dong quai, nettle and oat straw.

VITAMIN K

This lesser known vitamin is essential for liver function. It aids bone growth and repair as well as increasing longevity.

Meat sources: eggs, halibut, haddock, sardine and liver.

Vegetable sources: green tea, kelp, nettle, oat straw, shepherd's purse

MINERALS

CALCIUM

Teeth. Regular heartbeat. Prevent muscles cramping.

Meat sources: rabbit, chicken, goat, halibut, sardine, haddock, pork, lamb, goat, buffalo, egg and turkey.

Vegetable sources: chamomile, plantain, red clover, flaxseed, horsetail, chicory, dandelion, nettle, alfalfa, burdock root, chickweed, kelp and lemongrass.

COPPER

Helps convert iron to haemoglobin and is essential for healthy bones, joints and preventing anaemia.

Meat sources: chicken, turkey, salmon, sardine, halibut, lamb, goat and ostrich.

Vegetable sources: sheep sorrel

IODINE

Essential for healthy thyroid functioning and metabolism of fat.

Meat sources: Cod, salmon, sardines and eggs.

Vegetable sources: calendula, tarragon leaves and rhubarb.

IRON

An essential mineral for production of haemoglobin and general body metabolism.

Meat sources: rabbit, turkey, chicken, beef, salmon, haddock, lamb and pork.

Vegetable sources: uva ursi, eyebright, kelp, licorice, catnip, cayenne, paprika, oatstraw, plantain, dong quai, milk thistle seed.

MAGNESIUM

Improves cardio vascular functioning and prevents the calcification of soft tissues. Helps dissolve calcium phosphate kidney stones.

Meat sources: turkey, beef, pork, chicken, rabbit, goat, salmon, sardines and halibut.

Vegetable sources: bladderwrack, shepherd's purse, dandelion, fennel, parsley, fenugreek, yarrow, raspberry leaf, hops and lemongrass.

MANGANESE

Only a very small amount of this mineral is needed but it plays a role in normal bone development, thyroid hormone production, blood sugar balance and healthy nerves.

Meat sources: goat, turkey, pork, chicken, rabbit, halibut, haddock and sardine.

Vegetable sources: ginseng, yarrow, catnip, peppermint, fennel, rosehip, chickweed and hops.

PHOSPHOROUS

Important for kidney function, nerve impulse transfer, normal heart rhythm and bone formation.

Meat sources: beef, goat, rabbit, lamb, halibut, sardine, pork and egg.

Vegetable sources: slippery elm bark, burdock root and rhubarb.

POTASSIUM

Potassium is important for the health of the nervous system. A mineral that plays a role in muscle function and regulation of water balance and heart rhythm.

Meat sources: rabbit, lamb, goat, ostrich, beef, salmon, chicken and turkey.

Vegetable sources: hops, horsetail, catnip, sage, skullcap and red clover.

SELENIUM

An important antioxidant that protects against pollution and cell damage from free radicals. Regulates thyroid hormones, boosts the immune and plays a role in prostate function.

Meat sources: rabbit, sardine, salmon, lamb, goat, beef, turkey and chicken.

Vegetable Sources: Hawthorn berry, alfalfa, sarsaparilla, yarrow, garlic, horsetail, yellow dock and chamomile.

ZINC

It is important to supplement zinc as it is vital in warding off colds and infections and since the soil in many areas is zinc deficient, vegetables have a lower zinc content, so a pet needs to eat many zinc 'rich' meats and veg to ensure sufficient amounts. Zinc also plays a role in mental alertness and regulating oil glands. Zinc accelerates healing.

Meat sources: chicken, turkey, pork, lamb, goat, rabbit, salmon, beef and sardine.

Vegetable sources: alfalfa, nettle, milk thistle, parsley, rose hips, chamomile, mullein, cayenne and wild yam.

CHAPTER 8

Vaccines

Back in the day vets held the belief that it was safe to administer vaccines to pets over and over again, however most vaccines are actually effective for many years, if not a lifetime and need only be given once. Vaccines contain many harmful ingredients and minerals which are usually added for preservative purposes and thus need to be used with caution and only when really necessary. Yet some vets seem to be stuck in the old way of over vaccinating.

After you read about some of the key additives in vaccines, you may want to ask if it is all really necessary if your vet is keen on vaccinating.

Aluminum

Aluminum is a prevalent adjuvant in vaccines, it promotes brain inflammation and is known to cause brain degeneration and damage to the nervous system along with neurological dysfunction. If that was not scary enough, it also disturbs calcium homeostasis and reduces the level of brain antioxidants.
Research done by UC Davis suggests that up to 40% of dogs show at least one sign of dementia.

Humans who received five or more flu vaccinations between 1970 and 1980 are 10 times more likely to get Alzheimer's than those who only had one or two vaccines – this was discovered in research by Hugh Fudenberg, MD. The gradual accumulation of aluminum and mercury in the body due to the administration of these vaccines leads to cognitive decline and it is no different in pets.

Thimerosal

This preservative is mercury based and is still found in veterinary vaccines despite the warning being sounded for many decades. Repeated studies have pointed towards the extreme neurotoxicity of this product. In 1967 a study in applied microbiology found that thimerosal in vaccines killed mice.

In 1972 Eli Lilly discovered that Thimerosal could be toxic to tissue cells in a concentration as low as 1 to 1 000 000 which is 100 times weaker than that of the average vaccine. In 1977 in a hospital in Toronto, 10 babies died when their umbilical cords were dabbed with an antiseptic preserved with Thimerosal. In 1982 The Food and Drug Administration (FDA) banned thimersoal from use in medical products; however, they failed to act on banning thimerosal from veterinary products despite considerations in 1991.

In 2006, US Davis published a study which indicated that not only was Thimerosal a neurotoxicant, it was also an immunotoxicant which could make the immune system vulnerable to microbes and other malevolent influences.

Most veterinary vaccines still contain thimerosal despite these and many other warning signs over the decades. Thimerosal would actually be redundant if vaccines were manufactured in single dose not multidose vials, but producing multi dose vials is cheaper.

Contaminants

Contaminants may be at the root of many of the adverse reactions to vaccines seen in pets. Contaminants refer to anything unclean, impure, toxic or poisonous that has compromised the vaccine. Contamination can lead to many severe long terms issues, e.g., cancer, leukemia and other auto immune related health problems.

Official checks of vaccines for contaminants only pick up well-known pathogens and are potentially missing a whole range of other chemicals and particles, as it is simply impossible to totally eradicate contaminants from vaccines.

Animal Protein

Let's think about how vaccines are actually made.
Disease micro-organisms have to be cultured and they are often cultured on animal tissues such as cow fetuses and embryonic chickens. It becomes impossible to isolate the virus for the vaccine from the animal tissue so it all is injected into your pet.

When humans eat animal products, our digestive systems can deal with the animal protein and break it down into amino acids, which our body can use. However, when injected into the bloodstream, the digestive system cannot work on those animal proteins and the body regards them as foreign bodies, which produces an immune reaction. After being vaccinated, the immune system has much to deal with (e.g., the actual virus, thimerosal, aluminum and contaminants) so the animal proteins may slip through the net and become absorbed into the body's cells. The immune system can still sense they are there and may attack the body's own cells (which harbor these animal proteins) to get at them–you can see where cancer, allergies and arthritis are born.

Ongoing studies show that the antibodies dogs produce after vaccination can attack their own cells in the thyroid gland and connective tissue of the heart.

The Green Stuff

No, it is not a contaminant, a heavy metal or some obnoxious ingredient lurking in a vaccine, it is not even injected into your dog, but it is very much part of the discussion–money!

In 2005 the global vaccination market was $6 billion and in 2012 it was $34 billion. Media hype about vaccines like the canine flu vaccine may make dog owners feel like they are doing the right thing in getting these vaccines. But when the dust settled, was canine flu such a big deal after all? It is all a classic case of problem→reaction→solution→ka-ching.

Dr. Ronald Schultz who is a veterinary vaccine researcher states, "Few or no scientific studies have demonstrated a need for cats or dogs to be revaccinated." According to the research done by Dr. Schultz dogs exposed to distemper, parvo and adenovirus remained protected anywhere from 1-11 years after vaccination.

"The results from this limited group of dogs clearly demonstrated the Norden modified live vaccines provided immunity for at least 11 years against CDV and CPV-2, " says Dr. Schultz. Some distemper vaccines last 15 years, found Dr. Schultz.

In response to this and other research, the American Animal Hospital Association (AAHA) Canine Vaccine Task Force evaluated the data in 2003 to find evidence that vaccines had a minimum duration of at least 7 years. In their next move however they recommended that vaccination every 3 years was 'protective'. However, Dr. Richard Ford, Professor of Medicine of North Carolina State University, said that the decision to recommend a 3-year revaccination schedule for core vaccines was totally 'arbitrary' and there was 'no science' behind it.

Vaccines are a significant proportion of veterinary surgery income and the big business to the companies that produce them as a whole, so they are bound to want to sell more, not less—"it's the bottom line stupid", as they say.

Vaccination is a tricky topic and while many studies suggest less is more, you will have to discover which camp your vet is in and which way you want to go in terms of your pet's healthcare. Now that you're armed with this information, hopefully you will be able to make a more informed choice about vaccines in terms of the benefits and risks.

NOSODES

Nosodes are a specialized homeopathic medicine which have been used since the 1800s.

Although they have been controversial even in homeopathic fields the evidence of their efficacy and safety are growing and there are many benefits, e.g., decreased severity and frequency of illness, being noted.

Nosodes are prepared via a process called potentization. Potentization is when the homeopathic vaccine is prepared by removing infected tissue or a sample of a nasal discharge from a sick animal after which there is lengthy process of succession and dilution using homeopathic protocols which render it safe to be used as a vaccine. This process inactivates the original disease and converts the material into a bioenergetics remedy which interacts with the body's energy field to stimulate an immune response. The nosodes, once prepared, become energetic blueprints of the actual disease.

The benefits are:
- Safe
- Easy to administer
- Can be given to puppies earlier than vaccines
- Can be given to pregnant mothers to protect puppies from disease from birth.
- No chemicals
- No additives and preservatives
- Can be given orally rather than injected

Uses:
- Prevention (Homeoprophylaxis)
- Remedial

Nosodes encourage the body to produce immunity and, although this can be hard to prove in the lab, there are numerous examples of nosodes that have been used successfully to prevent and to cure.

Dr. Isaac Golden of Australia has done extensive research in the use of nosodes on children, finding that they are 90.4% effective. Dr. Golden published his research in a seminal book called 'Vaccination and Homeoprophylaxis: A Review of Risks and Alternatives', and 'Homoeprophylaxis: A Ten Year Clinical Study'. He found that children vaccinated with conventional vaccines were 15 times more likely to get asthma, 7 times more likely to get eczema and twice as likely to get allergies.

Homeoprophylaxis was used in a large scale outbreak of Leptospirosis in Cuba in 2007. Two million people in high risk areas received the vaccine and the data showed that the incidence in the areas fell below the historic mean. The results indicated that Homeoprophylaxis was effective in controlling the disease.

Another case was in 1974 in Brazil where homeopathic remedies were used to control an outbreak of Meningococcal disease. Of the 18,640 children who received the homeopathic vaccine only four cases were reported, indicating a 95% rate effectiveness. Of the 6340 children who did not get the vaccine, 32 contracted the disease.

Dr. Christopher Day, a homeopathic vet in the UK has been using nosodes for 35 years and has seen decreased rates of distemper, hepatitis, leptospirosis, parvovirus and kennel cough. In 1985, Dr. Day did a kennel cough trial involving 214 dogs in day care. The nosodes were placed in the drinking water. Some dogs had been vaccinated and some had not been. Only 1.9% of the dogs developed kennel cough, and the ones that did contract it exhibited only minor symptoms. Of the unvaccinated dogs, only 0.7% showed symptoms and of the vaccinated 4.7%. This goes to show that nosodes protect against the dog developing the disease and reduces the severity even if a dog does become infected.

The safety and efficacy of vaccines are being questioned as more and more studies link them to autoimmune diseases, cancer, allergies and other health issues. Nosodes are safe and easy to use as they are sweet tasting and can be placed on the gums.

So far, the results of nosodes are so impressive that they warrant some detailed research, study and data collection. They are safer, cheaper and possibly more effective than current vaccines and they have no long-term side effects and they deserve a serious chance to become mainstream.

CHAPTER 9

So, How Effective is All This Anyway?

Many things can be said about alternative medicine, both positive and negative. Many people do not believe in it and would never dare touch it, even if their lives were hanging by a thread. Others will swear by it and they have been using alternate remedies to cure many ailments of their own and of their pets. Around the globe, controversy has been raising concern about the effectiveness of these natural remedies. Some feel that they are not safe while others argue about their ability to cure diseases.

In the case of animals, most pet owners feel that these remedies are not strong enough as compared to western medicine. The truth is, these types of natural remedies are as effective as conventional medicine. We have seen many veterinary officers using a combination of both to treat and cure diseases in animals. Just because they are natural doesn't meant that they are ineffective.

So, How Safe and Effective is Alternative Medicine?

The fact that millions of people in Western countries are exploring alternative medicine as part of their medical care should ease your mind. This is to say that if they are safe for human use, why wouldn't they be safe for pets? The main reason is that people and animals having been facing some life-challenging illnesses that require alternative therapies, especially in cases where conventional medicine offers minimal help.

Just like human beings, animals are also affected by chronic illnesses that may require special medical care. However, there are cases in which use of conventional medicine may increase complications. These drugs are made of chemicals that may not augur well with some diseases. In such cases, alternative medicine becomes the only option.

As explained earlier, alternative medicine involves several medical therapies. For example, use of herbal medicines to treat different ailments in pets has been seen as a safe and effective method. Medicinal herbs can provide natural and safe remedies to some common ailments affecting pets. For example, aloe vera is used to heal skin irritations, burns, skin infections, and help speed up the process of wound healing. Ginger is an excellent tummy healer; milk thistle protects the liver against damage and improves its overall function. They are all-natural and, although they might cause some body reactions, their effects are much less harmful.

Use of holistic treatment has also been a major breakthrough in the veterinary community. Acupuncture is an important healing tool for pets, as it is with human beings. It helps treat or improve health conditions such as arthritis, degenerative joint diseases, hip dysplasia, asthma, and other health problems.

These are some of the great benefits of using natural remedies to treat your pet and improve its health. Apart from treatment, there are various natural dietary supplements that are incorporated with natural foods to promote healing and improve overall wellbeing. The fact that natural products are used in this case makes it even safer for pets.

Although scientists are yet to agree that alternative medicine is safe and effective, it is obvious the medicine has numerous advantages.

One of the health benefits of alternative medicine is that it helps improve the pet's overall health. This is because such remedies contain natural substances that promote cell regeneration and improve organ function.

The medicine also helps in boosting animals' immune systems. For example, some dietary supplements and herbs contain natural ingredients that help increase the body's ability to fight off diseases.

Holistic medicine also helps relieve pain, especially acupuncture (which helps ease chronic pain conditions such as those caused by cancer, arthritis, and other ailments). Acupuncture helps restore a balance of energy in the body and improves the overall health of the pet. Therefore, such remedies produce long-term results, as compared with the quick fixes that conventional medicines provide.

Alternative medicine also helps heal gastrointestinal problems which are the major causes of weight loss, loss of appetite, hair loss and general weakness in pets.

The benefits of alternative medicine are numerous. As a pet owner, you should be able to take full advantage of holistic medicine for the benefit of your companion's health.

No matter how effective alternative medicine is, there can be the side-effects, just like with all types of drugs. However, this should not be a cause of worry because as long as care is taken when administering these types of medicine and therapies, health complications are minimal. The fact that they also do not contain harmful substances makes them safer to use. The only common problems associated with use of alternative medicine in pets are allergic reactions, drug interactions, and confusion when extracting these remedies, especially the herbs.

Allergic reactions to certain types of herbs and dietary supplements are very common. To prevent such cases, it's highly advisable to get your pet tested by a professional vet. In addition, it's advisable to use alternative medicine separate from conventional medicine because they might cause interactions, which may severely affect the animal's internal organs.

All in all, alternative veterinary medicine has continued to gain popularity in the West as more people are becoming informed on the health benefits to their pets. These therapies and medicines have been used for centuries and have a reputation of being safe to use. Although many veterinarians find them unsuitable for use on animals, they have still proved their effectiveness. The good thing is that they are also readily available and cheaper compared to using modern medicine to treat chronic illnesses. Hopefully, more future research will shed significant light on the real benefits of holistic medicine and therapy.

CHAPTER 10

Strategies for Pets with Different Ailments

This chapter will help you track progress of your pet's health much more easily. It will help you identify those common signs and symptoms that might be a sign of an underlying problem. Identifying these symptoms may help save your pet's life.

This section will also help you master the necessary skills and even help you identify new strategies and techniques that might be useful to help track your pet's health progress.

Identifying disease signs and symptoms in pets

Some signs are simple to identify while others are just complicated. It's your duty as a pet owner to master your skills in identifying these problems early. Different diseases have different symptoms. Identify them and write them. Some of the most common signs and symptoms include:

Vomiting and Diarrhea	Constipation
Skin Infections	Allergies
Muscle Weakness	Gastrointestinal Problems
Weight Loss	Lack of Interest
Loss of Appetite	Anxiety
Frequent Urination	Fatigue
Increased Thirst	

If there is a possibility that your pet might be having some of these symptoms, tick them appropriately. This will help you continue to monitor your pet and identify what it might be suffering from.

Keep track of the situation while you notice which the signs and symptoms persist. Make a list of the number of occurrences and specific time when they occur. For example, you can write each symptom and the specific time they occur i.e. after meals, after exercise, after certain types of food.

Testing and Treatment

After you have identified the problem, testing and treatment should begin. Your vet should be able to test and identify the specific ailment. You and your veterinary can then decide which way forward and you can use this book to see if any holistic, alternative or diet related therapies could be helpful. Remember, it is YOUR pet, the vet sees 100's of pets and he cannot know them all as well as you do and so you can act as a detective to find the less obvious signs and symptoms your pet may be experiencing i.e. allergies and food intolerances which the vet may miss and which may be vital in addressing health issues and deciding on alternative, conventional or a combination of treatments.

Always keep a record of your pet's treatment start date, dose, as well as its response to the medicine. Responses might include possible side-effects. Continue with the treatment unless instructed otherwise. It's very important to report any unusual responses to your veterinarian immediately. It's good to know that most animals responds well to treatment within a certain period of time which depends on the type of disease and medication. In the cases of usual side-effects like itchiness, you may ask your veterinary for advice on alternatives.

Diet and Supplements

During treatment, diet is very important. There are various dietary supplements that can help promote healing. Such supplements include natural multi-vitamins which promote healing and improve overall health. Essential fatty acids that are important in promoting healing and better growth, and other vital supplements which also help boost the immune system.

Providing your ailing animal with natural foods helps them gain important nutrients that are vital in promoting healing. Create a weekly meal program and ensure that the diet is well-balanced.

Along with diet, ensure that your pet is getting alternative therapies which help reduce pain and speed up the healing process. Schedule a weekly visit to a holistic vet for acupuncture sessions, homeopathy, and chiropractic treatments. You can schedule a three days a week or even more.

Grooming and Handling

Bathing should be done at least once a week in the case of dogs. The hair must be brushed frequently to prevent matting, and keep the coat healthy. Always ensure that your hands are clean when handling a sick pet to avoid further contaminations that may lead to infections.

Exercise

Your pet must be properly exercised to speed up the healing process. However, care should be taken to avoid injuries. Schedule at least 30 minutes of exercise every day. Exercise should target the muscles and the skin to stimulate proper blood flow.

Weight Management

During times of sickness, there is a high chances of over-feeding your pet. This might cause a lot of weight gain. Being overweight can prevent normal healing, especially when injuries like bone breakages are involved. A healthy diet and proper exercise are essential during such times.

Rest

Your pet should have a good rest, at least 10 hours of sleep. This should be in a clean, dry, and warm place.

Socializing

Socialization should be done with limitations. Exposure to other pets might worsen the condition. A clean environment is also vital is such cases.

Understanding Behavioral Problems

Your pet may change behavioral patterns due to the illness or the resulting side-effects of the medicine. It's good to identify any changes in behavior and find the right strategies to control them. Some behavior changes may signify serious underlying problems that may not have been identified.

Understanding the Effects of Alternative Medicine for Your Pet

Tracking the progress of your pet's health means that you are well aware of the effects caused by the use of alternative medicine. Keep track of the shots and dosages given per day and record any side-effects shown. This workbook should help you develop the right skills and practices on how to use alternative medicine effectively to cure your pet from ailments.

A calendar is very important to help you track your pet's progress on a daily basis. Write down everything that your pet does each day.

Thank you so very much for purchasing this book, I do hope that it has been a valuable introduction to alternative health care for pets and can give you some ideas about how to proceed safely with these natural cures and remedies.
Always consult your vet or alternative pet care specialist.

Thank you to Sheebies, George, Dexter and Puppy for featuring in this book.

Printed in Great Britain
by Amazon